# ONE HUNDRED

# Words of

# Motivation

MARILYN E PORTER

**ISBN** 978-1-7338696-7-6

# ONE HUNDRED

# WORDS OF

# MOTIVATION

Printed in The USA 2020

# TABLE OF CONTENTS

# A MOTHER'S LOVE

## NANCY WINNINGHAM

A mother's love is from the moment of
conception.
A mother's love is needed when her child shows
some deception.

 A mother's love is shown when her child
requires correction.

A mother's love is when she teaches her child
right from wrong.

A mother's love is always strong.

A mother's love will never leave her heart
because she was there from the start.

A mother's love makes her give her all.
A mother's love will be there anytime her child
falls.

A mother's love will allow her to spend all the
money she has.

A mother's love will forever last.

# GRATITUDE

## THOMIAS HUGHES

At a young age I learned that instances in life aren't intended to be taken for granted. During my 20 years of existence on earth it's been a whirlwind of an experience. My mom once said, "I can back, but I don't have to go back." I've learned challenges are meant to make you a better human being and it allows one to evolve. It also makes your struggles and trials so beautiful, life changing, and it demonstrates why God puts you in the storm, goes through it with you, and gratitude is rendered in the midst of it all.

# SUCCESS IN THE MAKING

## TREVION WALTON

Success doesn't come without failure. If you're afraid to fail, you are incompatible for success. Your motivation, commitment, hard work and consistency is what it will take for your dreams to become a reality. Being willing to learn from your mistakes and having the ability to maintain focus after you've failed, takes strong character. You may fall six times, but you will get up seven. The greatest inventors, athletes, actors and entrepreneurs were great because they never lost hope and never gave up. Great individuals pursue the next opportunity to defeat failure and become a triumphant symbol. Stay the course!

# PURPLE BUTTERFLY WINGS

## SONYA MCKINZIE

When I was Young, Older, and in Between

I didn't see Beauty,

I didn't see Gifts,

Awakened by His Presence

I am Shifted

Unaffected by the World

I am Silenced in Serenity's Space

The Place where Peace resides

I am in Position

Transformed into His Invention

I am Silenced in Serenity's Space

Purposefully Born

I am a Butterfly

I am a Planted Seed

That Grows like Flowers

In Earth,

His Masterpiece

I am Adorned

He gave me Purple Butterfly Wings

Placed in Grace

Proof of His Affections and unconditional love

Validation that Jesus Christ

And God's Mercy Lives

# STRENGTH IS IN YOUR SEASON

## JE TAUN BARRON

All seasons are new and new brings forth change, change that at times creates uncomfortable challenges. It's ok to feel stretched, to fall, to bend to your limits, to become limp from exhaustion. It's Ok not to understand why you're going through it.

 We must not forget that during your season, there is purpose. Purpose to your journey, purpose to your struggles, purpose to baffling riddles with answers that cunningly escape us every time we get near. Purpose.... to what may appear at times, so purposely purposeless. Like the jokes on you, huh? The Devil is definitely a Liar!! Keep Going!

# BE ENCOURAGED

## JOY ZEISET

Just want to motivate all who are hurting and so many things are happening in their lives right now. Be encouraged and God will make all things beautiful in its time. The greater the pain, it is an indicator of purpose upon your lives. There are lives assigned to you by God for you to motivate and transform. So, nothing will be wasted, all your pain is reproducing a greater product. So, count it all joy when you suffer for righteousness sake. The scripture says your labor is not in vain. Be of good courage and stay motivated and build-up. Even when times get hard, stay steadfast. All things are working together for good for those who love God and called according to his purpose.

# YOUR GIFTS

ANNETTE WATSON - JOHNSON

Be encouraged and use the gifts that God blessed you with. If you know that you are gifted in leadership, prophesy, mentoring, finance, teaching, preaching etc., let God use you to encourage others. Use your gifts for the good of your family, business and community. Per 1 Corinthians 12:4-7 "Now there are varieties of gifts, but the same Spirit; and there are varieties of service, but the same Lord; and there are varieties of activities, but it is the same God who empowers them all in everyone. To each is given the manifestation of the Spirit for the common good".

# DEATH

THERESA LAWRENCE

Oftentimes when we hear the passing of someone, we love it's very normal for us to feel sad and even angry. Jesus wept before He rose Lazarus from the dead. One thing we all must face in life is death. According to John 3:16, God promised us eternal life by believing in Jesus. The last enemy to be put away was death, the Bible says. So, before a loved one leaves this earth, be sure they know Jesus because their soul will be everlasting, have peace knowing God gives eternal life for those who believe. Earth has no sorrow, that heaven cannot heal.

# GET YOUR MOJO WORKING!

## LOIS WAGNER

I have had so many challenges in my life: an abusive father; a serious childhood illness; divorce; hiking, scuba diving, and other adventure accidents; a violent attack and rape; a business going into liquidation; a six month debilitating back problem; losing everything I owned; retrenchment; forced retirement.

I thrive because I develop my mojo, my positive spirit, my joy and energy.

I live in the present moment.

I start from the inside, looking after myself, my self-awareness, beliefs, mind, body, heart and soul.

This positivity radiates to the outside where I project and present myself to the world with passion.

# ATTRIBUTES OF LIVING FREE

## FAITH WALTON

1. Confidence: When you start believing in yourself, you won't care about what other people think.
2. Believe: Hoping and wishing is one concept but believing it can happen is most important.
3. Wish: You can wish for God to do things, but you need to put your effort in also.
4. Trust: Be watchful with those you trust.
5. Renew: Stop looking in your past; look towards your future.
6. Love: Love isn't just an action word; it's an emotion that shows feelings, attachment, and happiness.
7. Forgive: Forgive those who have wronged you, so you can LIVE FREE!

# SURVIVE AND THRIVE

LOIS WAGNER

Develop your grit and resilience and restore your mojo to thrive after adversity using the ABC's.

- Accept Adversity. Feel it, rate it, stay with it for a while, then replace the negative emotion with a positive one

- Believe in yourself and your abilities

- Understand the Consequences, take Courage, and move out of your Comfort Zone

- Discuss, Debate, and Do something Different

- Energize and Empower yourself

- Focus on your aspirations and Follow Through with passion, perseverance, and persistence

- Get back up and demonstrate Gratitude

Pick yourself up.

Learn from your mistakes.

Forgive yourself.

Laugh.

Carry on with renewed determination and vigor.

# TO MY RAPIST

## LOIS WAGNER

I do not condone what you did.

You hurt me physically, emotionally, and financially.

I am choosing to be free of this pain and discomfort.

I release all demands and conditions on you and your life.

I send forgiveness with love and compassion from my Higher Self, that part of me that has protected me, loved me and nurtured me. And I send it to you just as you are and have been, and I release you to your highest good.

I accept back my power to express love and goodwill in a healthy way.

I TAKE BACK MY FREEDOM.

# WATCH WHAT YOU SAY!

## KEYWANA WRIGHT

Words are powerful, be careful what you say! Choose your words wisely. "The tongue has the power of life and death, and those who love it will eat its fruit". (Proverbs 18:21) This is true whether you are speaking of spiritual, physical or emotional things, into the atmosphere. Choose to speak life today. "A gentle answer turns away wrath, but a harsh word stirs up anger". (Proverbs 15:1) Are you a peace marker? "The Lip of truth shall be established forever; but a lying tongue is but for a moment". (Proverbs 12:19) Speak Truth!

## A BEAUTIFULLY BOLD BUTTERFLY

### LOIS WAGNER

We are all meant to become butterflies.

Like the butterfly we can transform from what appears to be death and can resurrect ourselves into positive symbols of survival.

We need to struggle to liberate ourselves from our caterpillar cocoons and emerge as butterflies with beautiful wings to carry us between earth and heaven, flying free from physical and emotional restrictions.

We can land on the flowers in the trees which are the embodiment of strength, beauty, wisdom, and eternal life. Trees are a symbol of a fresh start in life. A tree grows old, but its seeds ensure its immortality.

# THE GOOD FIGHT OF FAITH

## DR. FAITH WALTON

What does it mean to fight the good fight of faith? Fighting the good fight of faith is opposing moral turpitude, standing firm on the promises of God. There's fear in fighting because struggle is often associated with pain and other undesired emotions. It's sometimes easier to wave the white flag rather than persevere. If you knew the end from the beginning, enduring the fight despite the pain would be reassuring. Reassurance that your labor isn't in vain. God has equipped you with everything necessary to win every fight. Faith is your weapon. God is your guide. **GO, FIGHT, WIN!**

# GRAB THAT OPPORTUNITY!

LOIS WAGNER

Life is filled with opportunities, both hidden and overt. Sometimes we must go looking for them and sometimes they just appear.

- Keep your eyes open, be aware, and pay attention to what happens around you

- Practice mindfulness, breathing techniques, and meditation

- Be flexible

- Have an openness to possibility

- Actively seek new avenues

- Trust your gut and take a chance

- Manifest opportunities with vision and aspiration setting

- Challenge yourself, your thoughts, your ideas and seek new directions

- Believe in yourself, your intuition, and your free will

YOU are responsible for your choices.

YOU can make it happen.

Go grab that opportunity!

# YOU CAN RENU U

## KATINA L. JONES

Encouraging words can mean so much when it's delivered at a time of being overwhelmed with anxiety, uncertainty and self-doubt. Sharing your testimony can be the saving grace for someone in that moment.

Sometimes it's hard to trust and surrender control to God even though the scripture says: Do not be anxious about anything, but in every situation, by prayer with thanksgiving and present your requests to God and the peace of God will guard your hearts.

Hold on, keep the faith and know that whatever you do trust and believe you can RENU U.

# FULL STEAM AHEAD

GENAE KULAH

Sometimes we need to take inventory of our lives and stop the motion of backtracking. Things and situations in our lives sometimes tend to cause us to question what God has said and what we know to be true. That is always going to be an area of conflict, because the battlefield is in the mind. Every morning we get up with new mercies, and a CHOICE to submit to God's plans for kingdom service or not. So, let's CHOOSE to put our hands to plow and move full steam ahead. Lives are at stake, and we've been CHOSEN for this.

# KEEPING IT REAL

## GENAE KULAH

What exactly does that phrase mean? To some it means to tell how you feel without a filter or doing what you want to do without thought to what another person thinks. But are those true examples of keeping it real? No. God is the ultimate example of realness as we can see in His word. In it He tells us how He feels in a direct and loving way and is concerned about what we think of Him. Keeping it real as kingdom women means we must live responding exactly as the Lord with love and concern for others.

# PRAISE BREAK

## GENAE KULAH

Have you ever had one of those days when you just wanted to smile?    Nothing spectacular happened, but you just felt joyful. You finally understood the meaning of the phrase "The Joy of the Lord is your strength."  You can conquer anything, because Jesus is your conquering King. Nothing can bring you down, because He is the lifter up of your head. You have nothing to fear, because greater is He that is in you than he that is in the world. You can dream big, because He will make a way. Now It's your turn. Get your praise on!!!!!!!

# YOU ARE

## GENAE KULAH

Mirror, Mirror, Mirror on the wall. Who is the fairest one of all? Some of us live our lives based on that question. We do not know ourselves, so we seek the opinion of others hoping for an answer. Then we become what everyone wants while diminishing who we are until we are no longer recognizable. Man is not the mirror we should look to. God's word is. In it we find out who He designed us to be. I praise you because I am fearfully and wonderfully made; your works are wonderful; I know that full well. Psalms 139:14.

# WILL YOU

GENAE KULAH

Will you make up in your mind to become the person God called you to be? Will you decide to stop letting other people keep you from your destiny? Will you do the work of self-discipline to balance your life? Will you commit to positivity and eliminate the strife? Will you see each day as an opportunity to learn more? Will you live a life of forgiveness not counting the score? Will you begin to see yourself as God's masterpiece of art? Will you love as God loves with an open heart?

Father, not my will but Yours be done.

# A PANDEMIC

MARILYN E PORTER

During the process of publishing this book of motivation, our country – our world, was struck with a virus we have come to know as COVID-19 or Coronoavirus. Many lives have been lost and life as we know has likely changed forever. The notion of social distancing and excessive handwashing has become the new normal.

As the compiler of this motivational literary work, I thought it only befitting that we reworked the book to include a little motivation while the world is in quarantine.

Our prayers are with the world and may the peace of God rest upon those who have lost loved ones to COVID-19.

Can there truly be motivation in such a situation? Absolutely my friend. The bright side of COVID-19 is that we have come together, moved beyond out differences and forced to realized that we are HUMANS, and what affects one, affects all!

Here's to the resilience of the HUMAN RACE!

Blessings

Marilyn E Porter

## GOD, THE GOOD SHEPHARD!
### EZEKIEL 34:30-31

In perilous times, like these, we need to remember God is our Good Shephard. I want to encourage you today to look to the Good Shephard (God, almighty) is with you. The Good Shepherd watches over his flock. He protects us and keeps us in perfect peace every day. The Good Shepherd is our provider, he provides for us daily our necessity needs (food, shelter, clothes, etc.) The Good Shepherd is our healer, he will heal you (mentally, emotionally, financially, spiritually, and physically) The Good Shepherd is our comforter he consoles the broken heart.

## REJOICE IN THE LORD ALWAYS: AGAIN, I SAY REJOICE.
### PHILIPPIANS4:4

Our world is experiencing much pain and suffering. People are dying daily, and bodies are being attacked with the COVID-19 virus. The bible tells us, there will be a time to be born, and a time to die. A time to weep; and a time to laugh, a time to mourn, and a time to dance. Finally, brethren, whatsoever things are true, whatsoever things are honest, whatsoever things are pure, whatsoever things are lovely, whatsoever things are of good report, if there be any virtue, and if there be any praise, think on these things.

MOTIVATION FROM JE TAUN BARRON

## STRENGTH IS IN YOUR SEASON 2

The Season will come to an end, a new one to begin. Choose, choose to Persevere. When you look back at the triumph of the Season you've completed. There's amazement that awaits you, accomplishments to accompany you, Courage bestowed upon you, Wisdom crowns you, Victory has become You. God is building you even when it seems like he's breaking you. Keep Pushing, Keep Going!!

Stay Focused, Stay Favored!!

# MEET

# THE

# AUTHORS

# NANCY WINNINGHAM

Nancy Winningham is a wife, mother, grandmother, published author, educator, and motivational speaker. She loves to share her testimonials of the goodness of God's everlasting grace.

# THOMIAS HUGES

Thomias Hughes is a student at the University of Memphis who loves to encourage, enlighten, and inspire others through his testimony.

# SONYA MCKINZIE

Lives in Georgia with her daughter and is the CEO of Women of Virtue Transitional Foundation, holds master's degrees in Human Services Counseling, Communications, and a Certified Life Coach.

# LOIS WAGNER

Lois Wagner is a traveler, survivor, inspirational speaker, certified Conversational Intelligence® (C-IQ) coach, and mentor. She inspires people with her storytelling to make a difference in their lives.

# JOY ZEISET

Amazon Bestselling Author and Health &
Wellness Coach and Mom. I love inspiring
lives. I help people lose belly fat naturally.

# KATINA L. JONES

Katina is a Life Coach, speaker and founder of RENU U, LLC – where she nurtures women from back to emotional health, after hurt and trauma has paralyzed them. Her mission is to restore them back to their God-given destiny.

# GENAE KULAH

Pastor Genae Kulah is a woman after God's own heart. She is the founder and fearless leader of The Word 4 Her Ministries – where is teaches and trains women in the way of The Gospel of Jesus Christ. She is a life coach, author and serves as the prophetic voice of The PPIC.

# THERESA LAWRENCE

She loves the Lord and encouraging others. She's a entrepreneur, now author, an insurance broker and line, women's choir, armor bearer and part of the core team for the Singles ministry. She resides in Chicago.

# JE TAUN BARRON

Jé Taun is the Founder of Perfectly Imperfect, a nonprofit organization promoting positive body image and self-esteem. She is a wife mother of three and loved God. She lives in Chicago. She is a model, motivational speaker, and enjoys cooking. Her passion is to encourage others.

# ANNETTE WATSON-JOHNSON

Author and CEO Annette Watson-Johnson M.A., B.S is the Founder of Dynamic Participators Enterprise Inc. and the GIRLS RUN THE WORLD IN PEARLS global movement.

# KEYWANA WRIGHT

Keywana Wright is an 8x Amazon Bestselling author and self-publisher. She is a mother, speaker, life coach, prayer warrior and magazine freelance writer. She also holds a certificate in Leadership in Ministry. She is a Certified Life Coach.

# TREVION WALTON

Trevion is a talented actor and artist with a gift of brining joy to those around him. Following Trevion                    of                    YouTube
https://youtu.be/ITePQww3MeM

# FAITH WALTON

Faith is a funny, outgoing, lovable, and successful teenager. She loves God, has a big heart for her family and others. She enjoys writing, constructing art and tinkering.

# DR. SHERIKKA WALTON

Dr. Sherikka Walton is a Nurse Practitioner/Nurse Scientist, who believes, "If I teach one, I will reach many." Her love for God and people enables her to reach diverse populations.

# ABOUT THE COMPILER

## MARILYN E PORTER

Mommy, minister, media mogul in the making. CEO and Founder of SBG Media Group and Senior Pastor and CEO of The Pink Pulpit International Convention of Women in Ministry. Marilyn is a highly sought out SUPER COACH – she specializes in spiritual and personal development. Marilyn is known for helping her clients achieve maximum success through unconventional methods and has penned the statement; "World systems do not work for Kingdom people!"

She holds a MS in Leadership and Management, BS in Psychology and had an honorary doctorate in Ministry Development.

As a speaker, she is sure to captivate audiences from the stage and the pulpit alike with her easy to digest but hard-hitting methods of teaching and training.

She has authored more than 15 books to date

# CONTACT MARILYN E PORTER

WEBSITE:

WWW.MARILYNEPORTER.COM

EMAIL:

THESCATTERBEAINEDGENIUS@GMAIL.COM

FACEBOOK

WWW.FACEBOOK.COM/MARILYNEPORTER

INSTAGRAM

WWW.INSTAGRAM.COM/MARILYNEPORTER

TWITTER

TWITTER.COM/MARILYNEPORTER

SCHEDULE AND APPOINTMENT

bit.ly/marilyneporter

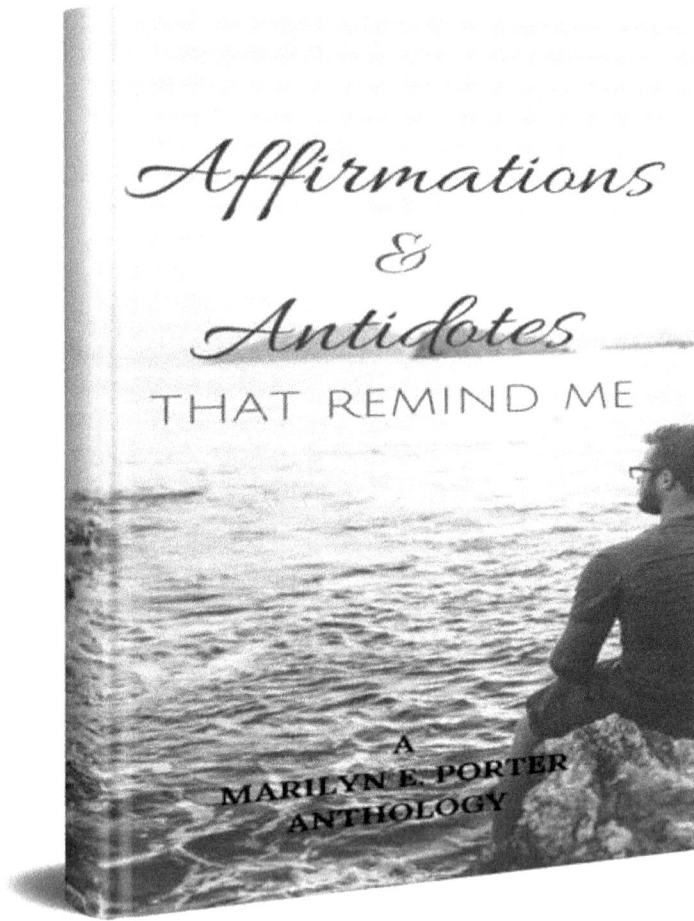

*Affirmations & Antidotes*
THAT REMIND ME

A
MARILYN E. PORTER
ANTHOLOGY

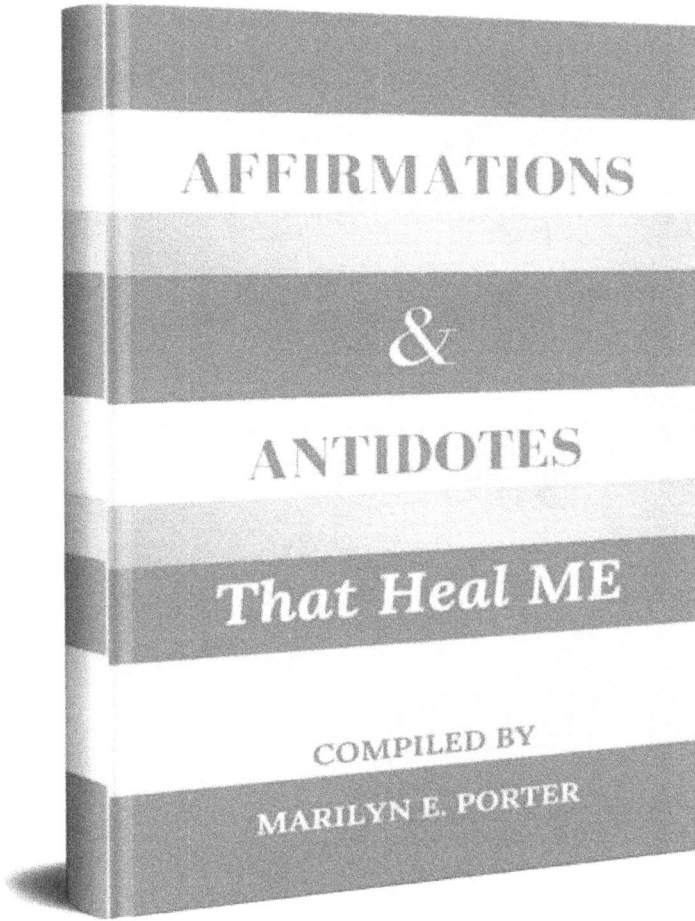

AFFIRMATIONS & ANTIDOTES That Heal ME

COMPILED BY

MARILYN E. PORTER

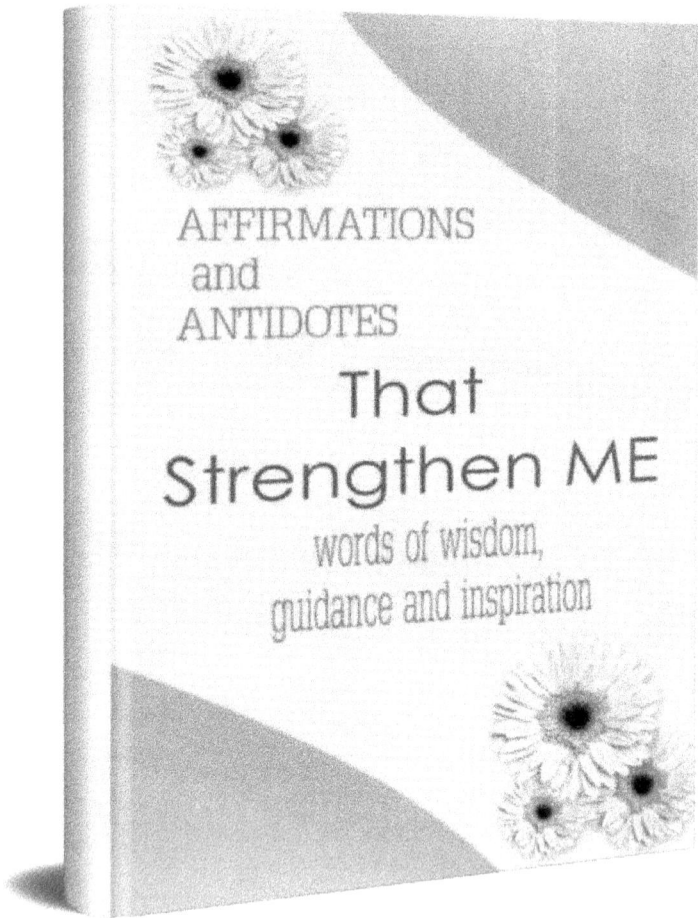

# FINALLY

To My Fellow One Hundred Words of Motivation and (Book 1) One Hundred Words of Inspiration Authors;

Thank you so much for you hard work and commitment to the project. Others may think writing a simple 100 words is an easy, but I know it is a task! I like to think that I am one who can do with ease, but the truth is that when I got the idea to write just 100 words to encourage, inspire and motivate others, I knew that I needed your help. And so again I say thank you from the bottom of my heart.

Blessings and favor be upon each of you, now and forevermore.

*Marilyn*

www.ingramcontent.com/pod-product-compliance
Lightning Source LLC
Chambersburg PA
CBHW071853020426
42331CB00007B/1986